STIR

 www.trafford.com

North America & international
toll-free: 1 888 232 4444 (USA & Canada)
fax: 812 355 4082

Thank you God for your faithfulness.

Foreword

You are probably wondering what this book is about. You have checked both the front and back covers (unless of course you bought the e-book) and will probably look again because you 'just don't get it'. There is neither an author summary nor a book summary and you are truly curious to find out what this book is about. This little intro won't fully answer that question, in fact this serves as a warning.

This will be unlike anything you have ever read; it will push boundaries and upset a few people. It will cause a riot of questions to be heard that we ignored and disregarded before. They won't be new questions, no; many thought of them before I did, but never gave voice to them. Why didn't they? Simple, they were too controversial. As a society, the church, and we its members don't want to 'stir up trouble', so we go along with whatever is 'trending', be it accurate truth or not. What we fail to remember is, if we stand on flawed facts and unstable foundations, our entire world will come crumbling down.

So I have decided to 'stir'. It isn't trouble I am stirring, but the truth, or at least my quest for it. However, all some people will see is trouble and resist what I have written on that flawed perception alone. They won't see what I am trying to achieve, the true purpose of this book. No, all they will see is someone challenging the current status quo and immediately deem it unrighteous, blasphemous, ridiculous...

Nevertheless, I will still write, and God will make a way for publication, because while some condemn, others will read, understand and ask the hard questions. The questions that need to be asked and answered; to save our societies; to deliver our children; to heal our sick and to grant our true salvation. The answer to your question 'what?' is; THE TRUTH. This book is about the truth, not what is popular or what is easy to accept, but the truth. It is the answer to a question that has been asked over and over, decade after decade.......

WHAT THE FUCK IS CHRISTIANITY?????!!!!!!

...STIR...

So.... yes, I said it. The 'F' word, boldly written in what is to be a book about God's truth.

Why not? I could have changed the wording, left that one word from the question and made it more palatable for some readers but why should I? If I had asked the politically correct question, would you be as interested as you are now? This question in its raw and naked truth is not only valid but honest. It is the question many ask in their minds even after the 'polite' question was asked and answered. It is the foundation on which our salvation is built, yet many Christians cannot answer it with a conviction that signifies they have a clear and true understanding. They repeat quotes they have heard, but these answers lack certitude, personal conviction and persuasion, because the speakers don't really understand what they are saying.

There are many opinions and definitions on Christianity. If you search the internet, results would include classifications such as; religion vs. relationship, fanatic vs. believer, Old Testament vs New Testament. The results from the search can leave you more confused than you started. Nevertheless, I continued my research and found a comment that appealed to me and spoke truth in its vague simplicity; *Christianity is based on the life and times of Jesus of Nazareth, The Christ* (Author unknown).

Vague but true. The simple fact is; there could be no Christianity without a Christ. However, that doesn't really say much, does it? It's an answer that would justify the 'Duh' response kids give when you state the obvious. It is the equivalent of saying, "the most famous equation of all time, devised by Albert Einstein" if asked what $E=mc^2$ is. Although true, it does not begin to scratch the surface on what it TRULY is or its importance and impact on the world.

We are therefore back where we began and faced with the options presented by many an author; religion vs. relationship, fanatic vs. believer, Old Testament vs New Testament. Many books and papers have been written, outlining these opposing views. They are portrayed as being so contradictory you have no choice but to choose one or the other. The arguments on both sides are so compelling you are forced to clinically categorise yourself and your beliefs to choose a side. But once you have chosen, something still seems to be missing. Doesn't it? So after a while you go looking again. Because the fact is 'there has to be more than this.' Your search for answers continues; the things you disregarded the first time, now seem to make some measure of sense and you are wondering HOW? How could some of the characteristics for a fanatic seem 'right' when you are a believer? How could religious rules apply to you, when your faith is based on relationship?

As a child, raised in a Christian society I went to church most Sundays; was a member of the choir; participated in church activities and so on. I gave my life to God at such a young age, I cannot remember when I did it, I just know that I did. I kept my virginity until I was married. I began praying and fasting in my early teens, didn't do drugs, didn't drink.

Was I perfect? No. Am I perfect? Hell no. But I do understand a truth that evades so many others. **You don't have to choose.** If both sides represent Christianity, how or why should you choose? When you do, it NEVER works; there is always something missing, something you can't quite put your finger on but leaves you feeling restless.

Some people go through their entire Christian lives with that feeling of restlessness. They love God and want to be all that He would have them to be, but the feeling never leaves. On the other hand, there are some Christians who have an inexplicable peace and acceptance with their Christianity. Which group do you fall into? Are you still searching for the ever elusive answer? Have you strayed because of your restlessness or are you sitting peacefully in your Christianity, confident that you are exactly where you need to be?

Search yourself carefully. PLEASE! We first need to be honest with ourselves about what we feel before we can achieve any resolution or subsequent 'greatness' in the body of Christ. If we are not honest, how can any changes be made? When you participate in any motivational programs aimed at putting you 'on the right track', the first step is always acknowledging (and sometimes voicing) the truth. In AA, participants first have to say 'my name is ... and I am an alcoholic/addict'. Self-help books ask you to first determine where/what the problem is, in order to confront it. Yet we as Christians think if we say and do the 'right' things; if we go to church every week and sing and shout God's praises, regardless of what we feel in our hearts; 'it's okay, God will be glorified and my family and I will be blessed'.

NEWSFLASH: It doesn't work that way. God works with honesty and truth (even if it includes a few 'f' words).

A father cannot fix a problem or soothe a hurt that a child refuses to acknowledge is there. Yes, God knows our hearts and sees the conflict and restlessness there, but what should He do? You ignore the nagging in your spirit. You refuse to go to Him and tell Him how empty you feel, to ask Him for clarity on something the reverend/pastor/ preacher said. He already knows how you feel and what you want to know; but who answers questions that aren't asked?

We meet people and see the hurt in them and the needs that we can sometimes fill but we don't always fill them. Sometimes, we're being selfish or lazy. Other times we tried. We asked and counselled but they refused to see and accept the truth, so we walked away, because... what else could you do? Why do you think it should be any different with God? We always forget, we were '**made in His image and likeness**', therefore, if you can't fix your friends problem although it is blatantly obvious, He can't fix yours. He can't soothe a spirit that you do not confess is restless, he cannot reveal truths if you do not ask the questions.

So ask. Talk to Him from your heart. Once you have finished being honest with yourself and God, **LISTEN.** He has provided answers. Whether or not you like those answers remains to be seen.

...STIR...

Relationship vs. Religion

In general terms the word relationship refers to the behaviours of two or more parties as they interact with each other. The type of relationship would further categorise the actions and behaviours of said parties. The Christian relationship, suggests a 'one on one' experience with Christ, the Son of God through the presence of the Holy Spirit. According to many, this relationship is not restricted by the dos and don'ts of religious laws. It is based on love and guided according to the glory of God and the wellbeing of the Christian. On the other hand, religion is seen to define the rules and laws laid out to be strictly followed for the service God. It is established and remains the same for all members.

As I said, so contradictory, you feel the need to choose one or the other, because, as they are, you cannot see how religion and relationship could possibly co-exist, but they do.

First, let me point out that the idea of relationship **instead of** religion was devised by Christians for Christians. It is the excuse we use to step away from the rules. It is the reason we have so many denominations and such discord among the body of Christ. It is the reason the body of Christ is in essence 'useless' in the ceaseless spiritual fight against the armies of darkness. There is tremendous power available to us through Christ, but many Christians have never seen and will never see this power at work because we do not want to follow rules.

"Most assuredly, I say to you, he who believes in Me, the works that I do he will do also: and Greater works than these he will do, because I go to My Father. And whatever you ask in My name, that I will do, that the Father may be glorified in the Son, If you ask anything in My name, I will do it." John 14: 12-14.

Where are these 'greater works'? My saviour doesn't lie, which leaves me to believe that WE have fallen short. We are constantly praying but very few see miracles. Why? What is lacking in us that we have yet to perform these greater works? The answer is discipline and obedience; the unwillingness to go through the process. For most recorded miracles Christ performed, there was a process. Whether he made paste, asked believers to take a dip in the river or the individual seeking the miracle having to fight through the masses surrounding Him, there was a process. Before the coming of Christ, the prophets also outlined the process to be taken when the Israelites needed to garner favour from God. So what makes you any different? We too need to follow the process. 'Lip-service' alone will achieve nothing.

When I refer to process and rules, I am not advocating those established by man, but the directives given by God. We have situations where an entire church came together and prayed and fasted for a particular result and did not see it. Why not? We brush aside these things and give platitudes like 'God knows best' but that is not good enough. Of course God knows best but His word also says **"Assuredly, I say to you, whatever you bind on earth will be bound in heaven, and whatever you loose on earth will be loosed in heaven. Again I say to you that if two of you agree on earth concerning anything that they ask, it will be done for them by my Father in heaven. For where two or three are gathered together in My name, I am there in the midst of them." Matt. 17: 18-20**

Again, the word of God does not lie, so the lack of results lies with the body of Christ. It isn't because 'God knows best' that we did not see our miracle, it is because we did not follow the process to see on earth that which was already granted/released in heaven.

Yes, Christianity is relationship, partially at least. Christ died for us after all. You don't do something like that for a people you don't know and love. He sent the Holy Spirit to be our comfort and guide, and as each person gives their life to God, and truly acknowledges the power and presence of the Spirit of God within them, their lives are truly changed. But with our Christianity do we ignore the religious laws God gave His people before the coming of His son?

"Do not think I came to destroy the Law or the Prophets, I did not come to destroy but to fulfil. For assuredly, I say to you, till heaven and earth pass away, one jot or one tittle will by no means pass from the Law till all is fulfilled. Whoever therefore breaks one of the least of these commandments, and teaches them so, shall be called least in the kingdom of heaven..." Matt 5: 17-19

The laws and rules governing the children of God did not disappear with the coming of His son. Two things changed when Christ came and died for us;

1- He replaced the altar of sacrifice. Through Moses, God gave the laws of sacrifice to His people, governing the means by which sin was forgiven, healing was received... and everything in between. These laws of sacrifice were not meant to control and manipulate the people but to guide them and allow them to see the rewards of God. However, when the LAMB was crucified on Calvary for our sins, there was no longer a need to continue these sacrificial practices, for the ultimate sacrifice had been made. **HALLELUJAH!!!!!!!!!!**

2- There was no longer a barrier nor a need for a human intermediary between us and our Creator;

For we have not an high priest which cannot be touched with the feeling of our infirmities; but

was in all points tempted like as we are, yet without sin. Let us therefore come boldly unto the throne of grace, that we may obtain mercy, and find grace to help in time of need. – Heb. 4:15-16

And thou shalt hang up the veil under the taches, that thou mayest bring in thither within the veil the ark of the testimony: and the veil shall divide unto you between the holy place and the most holy. – Ex. 26:33

Jesus, when he had cried again with a loud voice, yielded up the ghost. And, behold, the veil of the temple was rent in twain from the top to the bottom; and the earth did quake, and the rocks rent; Matt 27:50-51

The sacrifice of our Lord granted us access to our Father. We no longer required priest to speak on our behalf and prophets to receive a word from God. We were all given the same access, all granted permission to approach the throne and commune with our creator.

The rules which God communicated through Moses and other prophets concerning all other things remain relevant. From the beginning God was in the habit of giving rules and placing 'restrictions' on His children;

And the L**ORD** **God commanded the man, saying, Of every tree of the garden thou mayest freely eat:** [17] **But of the tree of the knowledge of good and evil, thou shalt not eat of it: for in the day that thou eatest thereof thou shalt surely die. Gen 2:16-17**

Consider what we have seen throughout biblical and secular history; human beings need rules and laws or chaos reigns. Mankind cannot exist without laws, hence the need for government legislations. So why are we so willing to accept the laws of man and not those of God? Why do we feel, that a God who regulates and restricts is not a God who loves us and one we want to serve? Don't you give your children rules by which they must abide? Do you love them any less for having to enforce such rules?

If you endure chastening, God deals with you as with sons; for what son is there whom a father does not chasten? - Heb. 12:7

It is baffling to me this need we have to follow and love a God who allows us to have our own way. Is that the definition of love? We want to believe that through our relationship with Christ and the love He has for us, we are exempt from having to follow certain rules that are not 'suited' to us. Why should you be exempt? Christ was a Jew and He honoured and respected the laws of the Jews. Yes, He made exceptions, or better yet compromises, but there is a huge difference between making an occasional exception and showing a complete disregard. A difference that the Christian community refuses to acknowledge. So what we as a society have done is moved from one extreme to the next. Are we any better off than they were before Christ came?

Christ came at a time when the laws of the Jews (religion) were so rigidly enforced that basic human kindness and compassion were ignored. Over the years, human beings distorted and manipulated the laws which God gave to Moses, creating a society so uniquely warped only the Son of God, and one of their own (a Jew) could show the error of their ways. He came to remind us of love and compassion, and how to incorporate them within the law, not to disdain what God the father requested of us. Yet, instead of seeing it that way, Christians have decided, that Christ came to 'abolish' or rewrite Jewish law (the laws of God, I remind you) and create a unique experience/religion/relationship by which we now abide.

Even if that were so, what is this 'new experience'? If it is strictly relationship based, why go to church on a regular basis? The relationship you have allows God to directly answer any and all questions you may have doesn't it? Why are there so many denominations in Christianity and which one is 'right'? Why should I believe what my pastor says when the bishop from my friend's church says something different? Should I...? Maybe if...? The Deacon said...?

This is why we need rules. This is why Christianity should be as much religion as it is relationship because without rules and laws there is confusion. Rules and laws provide clarity. We know what must be done and how, to receive certain results. We also know what should not be done and the possibility of punishments/consequences when we ignore.

Jews do not question Judaism, neither do Muslims question Islam, the way Christians question Christianity, because it is all quite clear. The dictates of these religions clearly state what must be done and how, so you make a choice; either follow the laws and be a member of the Jewish/Muslim community or don't and leave. Simple. Some small variations exist due to the passage of time but not on the scale seen in Christianity. How many variations of Judaism or Islam exists? Now compare this number with the variations of Christianity in existence.

Even worshipers of Satan follow strict rules and guidelines. Yet Christians are all about creating 'new' churches and denominations when we disagree with something being taught, or the way certain things are done.

Don't misunderstand, Christ did teach and reiterate the importance of **compromise** born of compassion, love and the glorification of God the Father. He repeatedly showed us the need for flexibility vs rigidity with the laws. I would never suggest He did not. But what we are doing today is not borne of compassion and love but a result of large egos and a lack of discipline. And that is a major problem with our Christian community, we lack discipline.

As members of a society, we will not agree with everything that is uttered from the mouths of our leaders. Truth is; every leader will not follow the mandates of God as they should, just as every King after David did not follow and serve God. I am not asking you to blindly follow someone you know is not of God, but I am asking you to trust. You have a relationship with your saviour; express your concerns to Him, pray for guidance and understanding as well as patience, seek to do what is acceptable in God's sight instead of what your ego and the egos around you demand. You **may** need to leave that congregation and join another or start your own BUT this has to be instructed by the Holy Spirit. Coming out of this relationship you have, God will speak to you as He did the prophets of old. Too often though, these decisions to move are based on slights we received; 'he was rude and dismissive of my ideas', 'she doesn't value the opinions of others' and the quotes could continue. We replace what should be the growth of the kingdom to another rift which needs to be mended. So what if she is a 'bitch' (You know you thought it. Didn't say it but we are being honest with ourselves. Right?), do you think that **Paul** was always easy to work with? Trust and wait. If God allowed them to assume the mantle of leadership, he will remove them if it is necessary. Just as He did the descendants of David.

Acknowledge and accept the laws of God. Follow the rules. **For certain men have crept in unnoticed, who long ago were marked out for this condemnation ungodly men, who turn the grace of our God into lewdness.... Jude 1:4** Through the coming and sacrifice of Jesus we joined the Jews in the category of God's chosen people. We did not replace them. Read your bible.

Christianity is based on the life and times of Jesus of Nazareth, the Christ. It is a religion tempered by the loving relationship between Christ and His followers who seek to glorify God with their lives.....

...STIR...

Believer vs. Fanatic

There is one word commonly used when demonstrating the fundamental difference between these two characterisations; extreme.

While both groups can be described as faithful followers, fanatics are often described as extremist. They are the group of believers, who follow the mandates of their faith, even to the extreme, with a blatant disregard for external consequences or opinions. They are usually considered to be obsessed and uncompromising.

Christians considered themselves to be believers. They consider fanatic to be a derogatory term that should not be applied to them and their faith. But why? Why can't we be fanatics for Christ? Why can't we do what he is calling us to do regardless of what the outside world thinks of us? Why can't we be obsessed with the mandates of God's word?

Presently, Christian believers are very concerned with the way they are seen by the world. We are very open minded and compromising on subjects we should not be; such as homosexuality and fornication. We use the aforementioned excuse of relationship as justification. But is this right?

'For we will destroy this place, because the outcry against them has grown great before the face of the Lord, and the Lord has sent us to destroy it.' Gen. 19:13

I have heard so many interpretations and explanations for this verse in order to justify and accept the continued practice of homosexuality it is appalling. It is quite self-explanatory to me. Where is the ambiguity to be interpreted? Why are reverends/priests/ pastors so accepting they are willing to conduct same sex weddings in the name of our Lord? **For certain men have crept in unnoticed, who long ago were marked out for this condemnation ungodly men, who turn the grace of our God into lewdness…. Jude 1:4**

..as Sodom and Gomorrah, and the cities around them in a similar manner to these, having given themselves over to sexual immorality and gone after strange flesh, are set forth as an example, suffering the vengeance of eternal fire. Jude 1:7

I am not saying Christ does not love homosexuals or lesbians, but is He accepting of their continued sexual practices? Similarly, we have Christians attending church on a regular basis yet they are having sexual relationships and are not married, but that is 'ok' due to the 'the relationship that person has with God.' 'God allows it (fornication) because of the place they are currently at in their Christian walk' or 'when they came to God they were already in the relationship, He will convict their spirit when it is time to end it,' **REALLY???!!!**

'Well shit, since sex before marriage isn't a sin for everyone maybe I should be a Christian too!' - The world.

Marriage is honourable among all, and the (marriage) bed undefiled; but fornicators and adulterers God will judge. Heb. 13:4

How is this not clear? Where is there room for compromise in this statement? Be careful, **for certain men have crept in unnoticed, who long ago were marked out for this condemnation ungodly men, who turn the grace of our God into lewdness.... Jude 1:4**

We came to God in sin and through love He accepted us as we were but changes have to be made once we make that step. Yet many of our sisters and brothers do not see the need to make certain changes immediately. They stay in their blatant sin under the guise of Christian relationship.

In what way is this service to God? When we open our doors and hearts in acceptance and disregard for the sins of our brothers and sisters in Christ who do we glorify? We so want the world to see the characteristics of a loving and compassionate God, an all-inclusive God, a God of unity, peace and love we compromise where we shouldn't.

'Do you suppose that I came to give peace on earth? I tell you, not at all, but rather division.' Luke 12:51

Again I ask. Who do we glorify with our compromising and acceptance? We need to ignore what others have to say once we are operating in accordance with the word and will of God. The things God calls us to do sometimes seem crazy or fanatical, even to us, but faith is about trust and obedience. Trust the relationship you have and obey the laws of the religion. This combination and careful **balance** creates a peace unlike any you have ever experienced.

When you ignore the outside noise and rest in the certain knowledge that you are doing what you are supposed to according to the will and word of God, there is nothing that can shake you. The internal restlessness mentioned before is non-existent. What is there to be restless about? You have the best of both worlds. The laws provide clear parameters within which to operate and the relationship you have with Christ allows the Holy Spirit to prompt you when an exception needs to be made.

It isn't 'easier said than done', it really is that simple.

The relationship we have with Christ tempers our fanaticism ensuring that it does not get out of control. It stops us from displaying much of the extremist behaviour seen in other religions. However, the discipline showcased by Muslims, Jews etc. is sorely lacking in Christianity. We are so concerned with the opinions of others and what is 'easy', we are constantly giving ground where we shouldn't in this never ending battle.

NEWSFLASH: The devil does not have to get you to serve him, he just needs to keep you from serving God wholly and honestly.

We need a little fanaticism. David danced before God, to the disgust of his wife and others, but their disgust did not change his resolve to show his love and devotion to God. How many of us today can say we have such resolve? Not enough.

Do you not know that the unrighteous will not inherit the kingdom of God? Do not be deceived. Neither fornicators, nor idolaters, nor adulterers, nor homosexuals, nor sodomites, nor thieves,

nor covetous, nor drunkards, nor revilers, nor extortioners will inherit the kingdom of God.

1 Cor. 6:9-10

Christianity is based on the life and times of Jesus of Nazareth, the Christ. It is a religion tempered by the loving relationship between Christ and His somewhat fanatical followers who seek to glorify God with their lives.......

...STIR...

Old Testament vs New Testament

Isn't this the same as asking, physical or spiritual? God vs Christ?

As Christians we cannot choose from the above. Our lives are based on the balance of both. We praise Christ for His sacrifice which allows us to serve God, in both the physical and spiritual realms.

Through careful study and prayer, the Holy Spirit has revealed to me that much of the Old and New Testaments of the bible say the same things one from a physical stand point (old) and the other from a spiritual (new). The coming of Christ re-introduced God's people to operating on a spiritual realm, and walking hand in hand with God as Adam did before he sinned.

There is therefore now no condemnation to those who are in Christ Jesus, who do not walk according to the flesh, but according to the Spirit. Rom. 8:1

Therefore, from now on, we regard no one according to the flesh. Even though we have known Christ according to the flesh, yet now we know Him thus no longer. Therefore, if anyone is in Christ, he is a new creation; old things have passed away; behold, all things have become new. Now all things are of God, who has reconciled us to Himself through Jesus Christ,

and has given us the ministry of reconciliation – 2 Cor. 5: 16-18

Therefore, there is no choice. Christians must accept and operate in both the physical and spiritual if they are to serve God and fulfil their purposes here on this earth. Our physical requirements cannot be ignored as we exist in the flesh. Yet the presence of the Holy Spirit forces us to acknowledge and operate within the spirit realm as well.

Our purposes in life, while they may vary in execution have the same end result, as we see in both the old and new testament scripture; **to bear fruit.**

'**Then God blessed them, and God said to them, "Be fruitful and multiply"....' Gen 1:28. "I am the true vine and My Father the vinedresser. Every branch in Me that does not bear fruit He takes away;..." John 15:1-2.**

We are to produce that which God can partake, 'children' to whom God can minister and be a part of their lives. When God gave the mandate to Adam in the beginning, they existed on a plain where daily communication was not blocked by sin. God would have been able to participate in the lives of these children directly.

When Christ spoke he was stating, we are not to quietly walk on in service to God, concerned only with our own salvation, but we are to be fruitful. We are to show the world who God is and what He can do. We are to demonstrate the love of Christ and draw others to Him.

What would be the purpose of having a fruit tree if it didn't bear fruit? It would be useless. It would be utilising resources that could be used elsewhere, by another tree/ bush/sapling which is producing, so naturally, we would cut it down.

Then he said to the keeper of his vineyard, 'Look, for three years I have come seeking fruit on this fig tree and find none. Cut it down; why does it use up the ground?' Luke 13:7

Christ sent us the Holy Spirit, not for us to horde and hide, but to show the world what is possible by God. In doing so, we draw others to salvation and bear fruit of; deliverance, healing and so on. God will not continue to feed your spirit with revelations and talents if you will not use them to fulfil your purpose. As Christ explained with his parable of the talents, God does not want back what He gave to you, He wants you to use it to gain more.

The 'first' Christians (the disciples, Paul and others), whose examples we frequently follow, did not forget the teachings of the Old Testament. They frequently referenced them as they extolled the name of God.

My son, do not despise the chastening of the Lord, nor detest His correction; for whom the Lord loves He corrects. Prov. 3: 11-12 & Heb. 12: 5-6

Christ himself also referenced the Old Testament in His teachings, addressing issues such as the religion vs. relationship debate at the same time.

And behold, a certain lawyer stood up and tested Him, saying, "Teacher, what shall I do to inherit eternal life?" He said to him. "What is written in the law? What is your reading of it?" So he answered and said, "*You will love the Lord your God with all your heart, with all your soul, with all your strength, and with all your mind' and 'your neighbour as yourself.'*" And He said to him, "You have answered rightly; do this and you will live." Luke 10:25-28

The Old Testament is the foundation which God laid to allow Christ to build the temple of love, sacrifice and redemption in which we now worship. Without it, what prophesies would there have been to fulfil?

Do not pick and choose pieces of God you consider relevant and present them to the world, for it is dishonest and blasphemous. It is also disrespectful and hurtful. Again, **we were made in the image and likeness of God**, do you like it when people ignore who you truly are and see you as they would have you be? Or do you prefer to be loved for the person that you actually are?

Just as we repeatedly reference scriptures from the New Testament, to point out the love Christ has for mankind, let us not forget those scriptures which show God to be a disciplinarian and warrior. A jealous God who is willing to allow His people to feel the pain and despair of persecution and bondage even as He is willing to come to their rescue and deliver them as they turn from their wicked ways and seek Him.

Love God for who He truly is. Serve God for who He truly is. Show God as He truly is. Stop showcasing and worshipping pieces of Him. Yes, He is a God of love and mercy. But He is also a God of war and discipline, among other things.

In order to serve God wholly and truly we must first acknowledge who He is. Read your bible and pray. Ask God to show Himself to you. For whatever we describe Christianity as, remember that Christians serve God; that is our calling as the body of Christ. That is the reason Christ came and died on the cross; for us to be reconciled to the father and serve Him in spirit and truth.

Our God is complex and as such our Christianity should be complex. The dynamics of our faith cannot and should not be easily categorised according to the headings many set forth. Each Christian is governed according to some basic laws yet, individual relationships with the Holy Spirit makes each experience different and cherished. We are not all called to call fire from the sky as Elijah, part the Red Sea as Moses did, or walk on water as Christ did and allowed Peter to do. Each life is different, therefore the expressions and portrayal of God by individuals is also different. Yet our purposes remain the same; **a ministry of reconciliation, to bear fruit which God can partake of.** By accurately demonstrating who God is and what is possible through our Lord and saviour Jesus the Christ, even in small, simple acts of humanity, we bear our fruit and further this ministry. All ministers are not called to speak from a pulpit but we are all required to be ambassadors, to display basic and common behaviours UNIQUE to God's people.

Christianity is based on the life and times of Jesus of Nazareth, the Christ. His example has fostered a religion tempered by a loving relationship between God and His somewhat fanatical followers (through the presence and guidance of the Holy Spirit). These followers, known as Christians, seek to serve and glorify God with their lives.

...STIR...

There remains one important characteristic of Christianity that seems to have been forgotten/overlooked by the 'experts' and authors. It is of such importance that Christ reiterated it multiple times in His recorded final prayer before His betrayal.

UNITY

"...Holy Father, keep through your name those whom You have given Me, that they may be one as we are." John 17:11

"I do not pray for these alone, but also for those who will believe in Me through their word; that they all may be one, as You, Father. Are in Me, and I in You; that they also may be one in Us, that the world may believe that You sent Me." John 17:20-21

How important is the concept of unity for followers of Christ, that our Lord and Saviour beseeched our Creator on our behalf, at that time. Yet here we are; Seventh Day Adventist, Pentecostal, Roman Catholic, Anglican, and the list goes on.

We have decided it is more important to; stroke egos and 'stand up for the truth'(the excuse so often used) than it is to; stand up TOGETHER for God; "**that the world may believe that You sent Me.**"

After Christ was sacrificed, the apostles continued to gather together, as the bible states, **'These all continued with one accord in prayer and supplication...''** Acts **1:14** On the day of Pentecost, they were not only in one place but again were of **one accord.**

'... they raised their voice to God with one accord and said:...' Acts 4:24 **'Now the multitude of those who believed were of one heart and one soul'** Acts 4:32.

I could go on with the biblical quotes but I believe I have proven the point. We constantly refer to the works of the apostles, the miracle at the gate Beautiful; **'And fixing his eyes on him <u>with John,</u> Peter said "Look at us." Acts 3:4.** What we do not place enough emphasis on is the way these things were accomplished. The process, the requirement; UNITY.

Saying the same words at the same time does not signify unity, the word of God says they **'were of one heart and soul'. "...that they may be one as We are."** This type of unity required goes well beyond holding hands and reciting a prayer together. It requires us to know, love and respect each other; to be honest with ourselves and our brothers and sisters in Christ; to ensure our individual goals are aligned with the 'universal' purpose. In essence, to open our hearts to each other, the same way we do for Christ and His Holy Spirit.

And the Lord said "Indeed the people are one and they all have one language, and this is what they begin to do; now nothing that they propose to do will be withheld from them." Gen 11:6

A people united can do anything. Add to that the power Christ gave to us when He died for our sins. Do you see why unity is just as important as faith and discipline for the Christian community?

When we establish new denominations or new churches because of 'in-fighting' whom do we glorify? When we sit in the pews beside our brothers and sisters every Sunday and lift our hands in praise and thanksgiving, yet refuse to offer simple greetings to each other because of some slight, imagined or not, whom do we exalt?

NEWSFLASH: 'To Divide and Conquer' is not a concept limited to physical warfare. Spiritual warfare utilises many of the ideals men think they devised. Remember; Satan does not have to get you to call him King in order win, he just needs to dominate you.

"If a kingdom is divided against itself, that kingdom cannot stand. And if a house is divided against itself, that house cannot stand." Mark 3:24-25

This is not a declaration implying there should be no disagreements amongst Christians. To make such an assertion would lead us to another extreme, where critical debate and beautiful creativity is stifled. However, the Bible guides us on the handling of disagreements with each other.

"Therefore if you bring your gift to the altar, and there remember that your brother has something against you, leave your gift there before the altar, and go your way. First be reconciled to your brother, and then come and offer your gift." Matt 5:23-24

Offering praise and worship from a heart that is bitter and seeks the humiliation, destruction or pain of your brother or sister in Christ is blasphemous. Christ instructs us to **"first be reconciled to your brother."**

NEWSFLASH: We need each other. If we did not God would not have created Eve.

Christianity is based on the life and times of Jesus of Nazareth, the Christ. His example has fostered a religion tempered by a loving relationship between God and His somewhat fanatical followers (through the presence and guidance of the Holy Spirit). These followers, known as Christians, stand united in their service to God and seek to glorify Him with their lives.

...Stir...

ARE YOU A **REALLY** CHRISTIAN?

Printed in the United States
By Bookmasters